WHAT THEY SAID

Story by: Allyn L. Howard

Illustrations by: Elena Adam

Author's acknowledgements

This story is dedicated to people who love animals. Especially to those individuals who devote their time, resources and love to homeless animals.

From the staff at animal shelters, to volunteers who foster, and the "everyday person" who will rescue a stray off the street....this book celebrates you! Proverbs 12:10

Illustrator's acknowledgements

To have a pet during one's childhood not only cultivates feelings of pure joy and happiness, but it also is one of the best ways to learn to be responsible, loving and caring for a creature that totally depends on you.

The moment you bring home a pet , it is essential that you tap into your own humanity and your sense of benevolence. The love you feel for your pet changes you, molds you and ultimately makes you and better person.

To the parents that understand this concept and are willing to accept all future inconveniences that come with adding a new member to the family; to all of the parents who opt to say, "Yes!", when their child asks for a pet...I thank you

A portion of annual sales of this book will benefit the
Saint Louis Scottish Terrier Rescue and the Virginia Beach SPCA.

One day a family went to the shelter to get a dog.

The mommy said,
"This is fun!"

The daddy said,
"Let's do this!"

And the boy said,
"Awesome!"

So, they brought the dog home

and they all fell in love.

But, the next day the
dog was so happy

to have a family
to call his own,

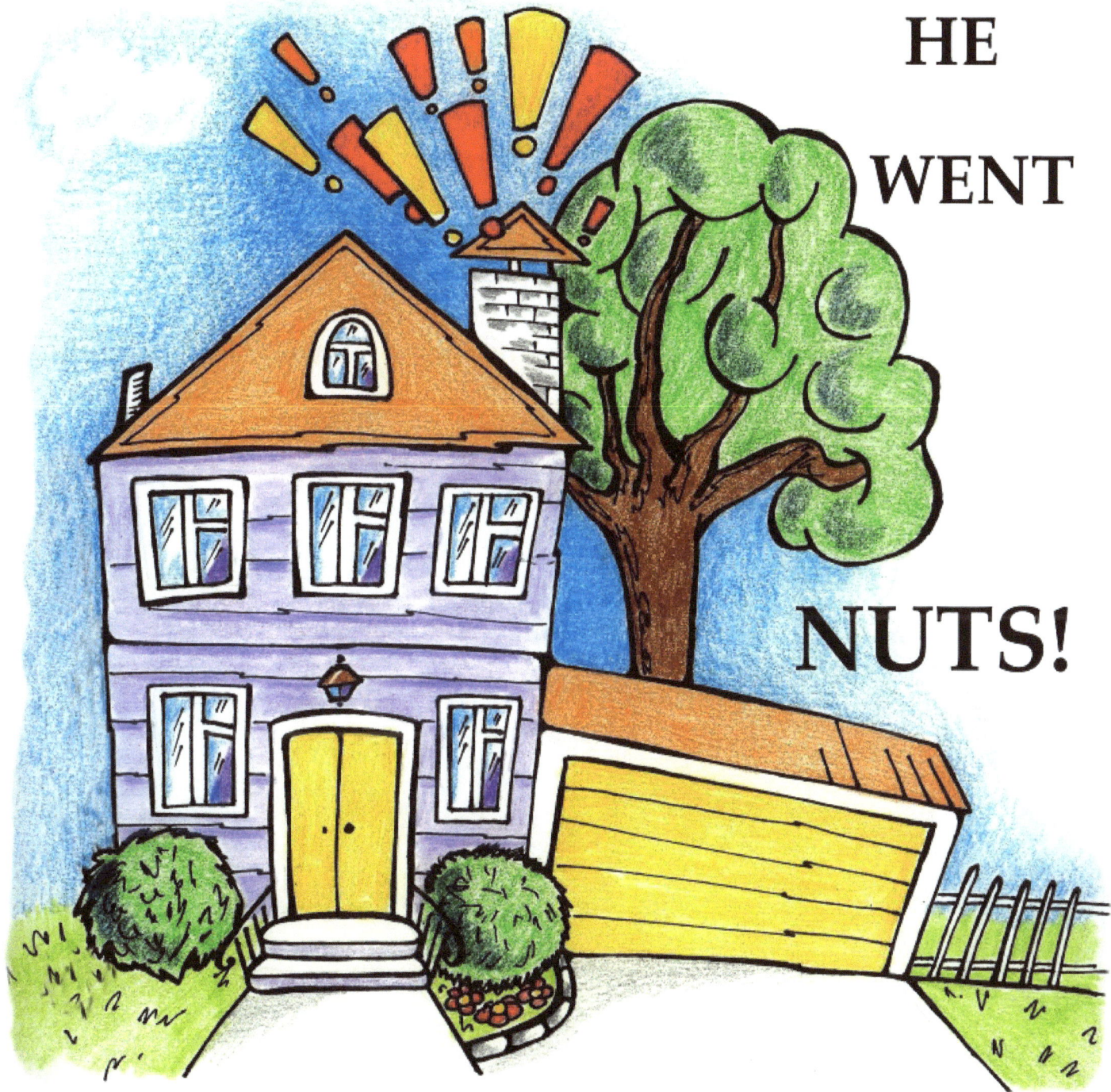

HE

WENT

NUTS!

The mommy said,
"Uh oh."

The daddy said,
"No, doggy! No!"

And the boy just laughed.

But with a little patience,
a lot of love and some training,

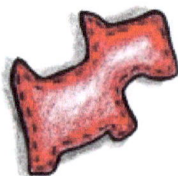

the happy dog got in sync
with his new family.

The mommy said, "Awww."
The daddy said, "Good dog!"

The boy said,
"You are my best friend!"

And the dog said, "Woof!"

One day a family went
to the shelter to get a cat.

The mommy said,
"It's time."

The daddy said,
"Whichever one you want."

And the girl said,
"That one."

So, they brought the cat home

and they all fell in love.

But the next day,
the cat was so happy

to have a family
to call her own,

The mommy said, "Get down!"

The daddy said, "Really?"

And the girl just laughed.

But with a little patience,
a lot of love and some training,
(well, as much training
as a cat will allow)

the happy feline
got in sync with her family.

The mommy said, "My sweetie."

The daddy said,
"Come sit on the couch with us."

The girl said,
"You are my best friend!"

And the cat said, "Meow."

Always make sure your pet has fresh
water and healthy food.

Never leave a pet in a hot car;
even with the windows down.

Give your pet a lot of fun and
pet friendly toys to play with.

Spay and neuter.

Shower your pet with patience and love.

Having a pet is not always fun and easy, nor cheap;
but it should be a lifetime commitment

Take your pet to the vet for shots and check ups.

SHELTER PETS ARE AWESOME PETS!

THE
END

ALLYN L. HOWARD has always enjoyed writing for the fun of it. It was not until her son insisted she write down a tale she made up for him, that she strongly considered sharing her musings and stories.

In the summer of 2015, her first young readers book, *Freya's Friend*, was published. Allyn, her husband, son and beloved dog, Harry, reside in Virginia. Harry, a rescue from the Virginia Beach SPCA, was the inspiration for this book. He was a puppy who needed a little patience, a lot of love and some training. Well, actually A LOT OF TRAINING!

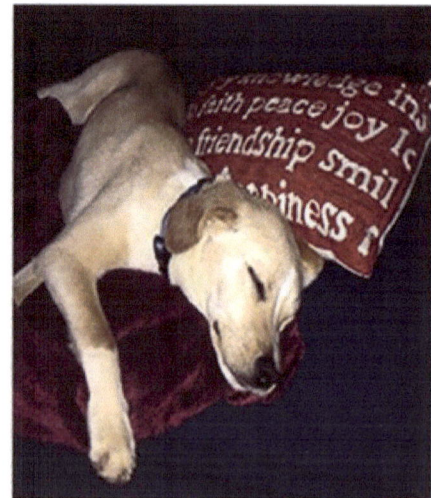

Harry

ELENA ADAM was born in Sumgait, Azerbaijan near the shores of the Kaspian Sea. As a child she liked to draw with colored pencils; which in fact today continues to be her favorite art medium although her portfolio now includes watercolors, oil paint and mixed technics.

A graduate from Moscow State University, Elena has worked on several newspapers and magazines as an editor, art editor and writer. In 2001, Elena moved to United States, where she continues to work as a fine artist and book illustrator. She lives in Michigan with her husband and beloved Scottish terrier Dussia.

Samples of Elena's extensive art portfolio can be viewed at www.elenaadamart.com

www.ingramcontent.com/pod-product-compliance
Lightning Source LLC
Chambersburg PA
CBHW041237040426
42445CB00004B/62